Lip

Lip

KATHY FAGAN

EASTERN WASHINGTON UNIVERSITY PRESS

14 13 12 11 10 09   5 4 3 2 1

Cover illustration: Lee Miller, Portrait of Space,
nr Siwa, Egypt (1937). Copyright © Lee Miller Archives,
England, 2008. All rights reserved.

Cover and interior design by Richard Hendel

Library of Congress
Cataloging-in-Publication Data
Fagan, Kathy.
Lip / Kathy Fagan.
    p. cm.
Poems
ISBN 978-1-59766-049-5 (alk. paper)
I. Title.
PS3556.A326L57 2009
811'.54—dc22
        2008054034

The paper used in this publication meets
the requirements of ANSI/NISO Z39.48-1992
(Permanence of Paper).

Eastern Washington University Press
Spokane and Cheney, Washington

CONTENTS

For A,

for my family and friends,

and for my students,

who give me plenty of—

Lip

Here lie the mawkish petty officers of cruelty.

Sulfuric pizzles on the bottom doggies of August's dog days.

Aristotelians on land and at sea in the Ministry of Miracle and Antipode.

A luster of wet cars signaling like sheep just queuing up,

        Before the morphine of the shrouded cliff.

At church, the homburgs keep cushioning the pews of St. Joe-Pye Weed, in felt.

The gist of opera buffa is its Neapolitan jaunt from the hilltop to the vernacular,

        Human stink curling from their campfires.

All of those lawless swaths running like jokes on the lam from the historical hoosegow.

So many solos striking out for the plains.

. . . .

It was a small stage.

                We knew

Every board.

                There were

Marks and shadows of

                Marks on

Wood warped thin and pale, like

                Us. Every fold

Of curtain

                We had

Darned and huddled in.

                Every shoe

And skirt hem

                Reeked

Of gas the footlights

                Burned. In clouds

Of sweat and tulle

                Backstage, we passed

The lampblack, lard,

                The tin of java

Rice, a single rabbit's foot we'd

                Filed the claws down

On. When a girl was ill

                We suckered up our

7

Spit for her onto a
                              Scrap of crimson
Ribbon, rouged her cheeks,

                              Stained
Her lips, imparted
                              Expression where none was before.

It was then I saw it best:
                              Doll. Whore. Clown. Corpse.
The perdition

                              We were threatened with.
They couldn't scare me with
                              Perdition.

I'd brought back
                              Souvenirs
From there I gave away.

                              My palms hold
The scorched smell of them
                              Still.

I prayed only
                              Once.
And when I prayed

                              Bitterness fled

In a black cloak
                              From my heart.
Without it, what did

                              I have.
It's autumn in
                              The Second Act.

Toward clouds hung, literally, in
                        The night sky,
Giselle ascends from

                        The tomb's trapdoor,
Right foot first.
                        Because the left hind foot is last

To leave the earth
                        We cut it off
And call it lucky.

                        Powder clings expertly
To each tine of fur;
                        We cross our faces

With the weight that once passed fleet
                        Across the faces of our dead,
And up

                        From Hades,
Warmly flicked a flea upon a
                        Chill and moonlit

Field. The stage lights caused
                        Our paste
To shine at times as if

                        Real moons
Shone in the true jewels of
                        Breathing

Princesses. I have it
                        In a book
That clouds be formed

Of dust and water,

Gems of

Dust and fire.

But greater than these elements is

Air,

Which looks

Like nothing,

And feeds these three

As I have been

Fed.

*"And I took the little book out of the angel's hand,
and ate it up; and it was in my mouth sweet as honey:
and as soon as I had eaten it, my belly was bitter."*
—Revelation 10:10

. . . .

When I took it from the hand it was not hand so much as cloven.
When I turned and faced the stars they rushed in closer to my eyes.
And though I tasted flame and stone then, I retasted wick and mosses,
And I heard a legion whisper, heard their heel upon the floor.
All the roses in the world then bloomed at once for me, and faded,
Like a light switched on, then quickly off. Thus I understood
The mythical contrasts, the secular hum, in which memory resides.

What I expelled resembled seed. We know the animal by its droppings,
Or later, at roadside, by a remnant of its coat, exquisitely
Intact. Likewise the willows, downed last winter, foam green on every
Whip, as if death meant nothing to them. They are godly. As was the cat,
Napoleonic at its window day and night. And at times
The pond shone like a mirror, yes; but you, you were the brighter thing.

In the beginning are
the sun, two houses propped
on their sides, an eyeball, one
deciduous tree, an inch
of fence, one fairy or
angel, an unusually small
evergreen. Smoke
lifts from one chimney
toward the eye, or smoke
scrolls down from eye to
chimney: you don't have to
choose.
After that, the
faces, a study in thoughts
of people I've met. One is dead.
Her face is the skull
face. More than one
is dead. I think more of them
all than they think
of me.
Finally come
the hatchet with its symmetrical
blade, the neck with its symmetrical
profiles on top, me looking
concerned because my arms are
longing and a snake
paisleys between my club-
hands and the crucifix I reach
for. The threat
is there
then as anyone can see,
as plain as the rabbit rounding
the tree trunk of your finger,
and I have difficulty drawing
a breath or anything
beautiful.

"God helps those who help themselves."
—peasant proverb invoked by St. Joan
at her trial

. . . .

So I lied & I fled & I prized
up the floorboards where necessary, yes.
For it was May then & the bells,
I kneeling in the light they made & would forever have.
But the lily was a sword with a cross inside it,
a voice in the bell of its throat.
What good I did because of them—
the rest was me.
The crucifix my confessor held so I could see
sailed like my standard, my beautiful peeling river,
Jhesus Maria blistering in the wind.
I felt I rode with it again—
times it raised me from my mount,
a vapor with arms.
Some say at the end my heart didn't burn.
People like their stories whole.
The truth I am not given leave to know.

Wind & warp, weight & paddle
& the sea in a box on my windowsill.
There's a gull on the roof—
I can hear it—

A gull with a goiter gobbling up the _____.
The gull is the roof & the thought of the roof
—if a roof had thoughts,
which it must, for it is the head of the house.

I am the womb of the house,
the womb at the loom! Monthly blood arcing
like the blood of an artery nicked.
Not that I've seen an artery nicked

except on TV. Not that I own a TV.
But in a way, I am TV.
All stance & no (sub)stance.
Nothing to feel & everything to comment on.

Jack Paar, Jack Kennedy, Michael Jackson,
Jack Off, a box of boredom with a toy
surprise ,,, ~ :>)
Which returns me, always, to poetry.

This is not a pantoum.
It may only be a shroud.
A Stein is a Stein is a
white space around the box

& the _____ that is the sea
raveling, unraveling.
Laertes dead for years.
I never weaved a day in my life.

When I cut
my blade was hardly red—
so little blood was in him.
Less spill than suck,
his wound worked like a mouth,
and mouth and wound alike drank
what I fed him,
my husband's father,
eyes fluttering like an infant's,
until I saw in them
the sated look that women
mistake for gratitude,
and saw too, beneath my hands,
a lustrous black returning to his beard,
a pleasing heft to thigh and shoulder.
What happened next
was strictly clientele—I'd always
been, as they say, in business,
exchanging life for life.
When Jason turned
us out to wed another,
it took no art of mine to kill
our sons. I'd loved
the magic for how it loved him.
I loved the anger for how it did not.

Relying on a Lethe-like result I pitched
my camp upon this riverbank. I drank.
And rather than the nothing that I sought got something
more, and far too often,
like laying down one's head
into the calls of birds: squabble, quarrel, fray.
Yet I stay.

Bears bed below my window,
as do the doe and her stiff stiff fawn.
At dawn their ginger ears flick off the dew,
the sun. They look me in the eye
as if I'd drawn a gun, and then do lumber,
and then do canter, but never
do they wonder.
Never.

O phalanxes of Pharisees,
pharmacopious phenomena,
all plenitude of you in the effluvia, hold forth!
Extemporate for me an explanation
for my wonderings why.
Try.
Here I am:

ears peeled, eye
to the ground, fingers worked to the
grindstone, my legs an open book. Book
me. Take me in, I pray.
And smite mine imagined enemies.
For I have seen to it
they were armed when they left here. Wild.
And I am become mild-mannered.
Unraveled. Reviled.

Am I wrong, or were you
the galoot who bitter, blighter,
scatter were. Were the dark
that dawned, that hit, that had me
rue the day, then duck, then hide,
then turn away. The bowls
of my hands made a seashell,
cracked, you could hear the ocean
run through, shell game,
shell shock, after-, electro-, -treat,
I mean wheat, shock of
copper where the penny's
nicked, your molars
human size but otherwise
exactly like a mastodon's.

Let's paint the town

        taupe,

let's wear our

        dental dams

and dance on

        eggshells

slick side down.

        We'll scrub our

cherry

        pinks off, we'll scrape

the porcelain

        back to its clay. Let's

break

        the day, shuck

my bodice,

        watch it husk

away.

Give it to me

        drily.

Dawn's tumbling

        in, her

lips frosted

        the nacre

of breast milk, dead

        tooth,

sea glass, an old

        corner

of your eye.

        You

might call

        the color

cadaver.

The doors of my town are yellow
like a canary
it would melt if you tried to
touch it like mother
love it would burn your hand it could
kill you is how soft and how yellow like
Sandra Dee's hair she
married Mack the Knife her
hair like pale butter next to his
full-fat unsalted
similes pale beside true poetry I'm told but
without them aren't we a hard and sorry
bunch like unripe bananas
like most all girls I wanted to be
like her bright as a newborn
chick like a canary in a mine
shaft like satin in the grave
the pale yellow things die first
in my experience Easter
the canaries of Woolworth's
the sign of the cross out
of the corner of my eye I saw her
make as the motorcade
passed slowly to our left how
bracing these yellow doors are
like a cool drink like
someone with his thumb on your
forehead like the light
that hardly ever happens anymore
every year about
this time.

On the urban grid of three PM she is
off it—the bus just huffing from the curb, she
lifts her backpack over her head, then brings it
down dead weight, full speed to the ground. By its straps
she heaves it up and down again. What's in it
she wants to kill? What's in you that wants her to
kill it? To KO the Collected Shakespeare,
the Xmas knitting, the kittens, the bloody
fetus? You want to help, help make it stop, help
make it go. But in the ritual movement
of three PM she is an errant woodwind
outside the score. Where did it go, the good you
believed was inside everything? She's thrown it
down. She won't carry your faith on her back.

....

after Dickinson

I cannot fly like bridges—
I am a looser thing—
More heavy and more useful
Than those who wear a wing.

I am a thing that slouches
But not without my form—
For those who fear a crossing
I can be crossed upon.

I have an architecture
If not the actual arch—
I'm cross-tied inexpertly
By juniper and larch.

But if it's reach you're after—
A thoughtlessness of loft—
Should Jupiter or Mars inspire
Your altitudinous lust—

Then do not think to lift
A foot onto the likes of me—
I do not love Your Highness
Though bow eternally.

The foot that feels the river
Intuits what my use is—
I tether the mortalities—
I cannot fly like bridges.

When the moon assembles the stars on the blue baldachin
And I am become the perfect center of one
Five-pointed star, the hole in my own crown,
Having seen the crown, Stephanos,
Gold in the blue atmosphere,
I will walk to my coronation
Amid minions of maple and beech
Who bow and bow,
Their young hair spiked in the cool atmosphere,
Gowns aroar like oceans in an ocean's shell.

At what moment will I first look up?
From what will I turn away?

In that rare atmosphere,
I will walk a path like powder underfoot
Through leafy mayapples—those excellent witnesses—
A cardinal ahead, the three queen mothers, my subjects' limber
Backs, lovely hair, a roar that dies down dies down,
And in awful light, I will accept
My scepter. The usual
Fanfare, the pink embellishments. Bells, trumpets.
Then will I be anointed by no one,
And serve him well.

He shall be green.
He shall boast a prominent
nose. The offspring of his
haberdashers shall attend expensive
colleges. His French
shirts wrinkle artfully;
his trousers never lose
their crease. He shall wear
a sportcoat of cashmere
the color of rotted lettuces.
Though he drape it
over the back of many
a chair and forget it,
it will always be returned to him
on the arm of a simple girl.
His cravat is every
color of the sea. Some say
he is a bird. Others compare him to
the frog. He drives
a Fiat. He is often late.
He was born, without fanfare,
in St. Louis. He was frequently
chastised. Otherwise,
his childhood was
unremarkable. His feet are
small for a man of his
stature; therefore, his shoes
are girlish. He snorts like a horse.
His interjection is *Ha*,
used to express wonder,
triumph, puzzlement, or
pique. Never surprise. He is
never surprised. He can dance
the habanera. His instrument is
the horn. Hydrogen is

his element. Narcissus,
his emblem. His laurel wreath
is a cowlick that sometimes
comes loose and trails
behind him. He is warden of
the 8th hall of the 2nd heaven,
the master of minor
pronouncements, grass
clippings, and some of the
waters of life. He will eat
a chestnut in any form.
He may be summoned only
when the invocant is facing
south. A certain song
from the '40s causes him
to weep openly. He never
remembers the tune's effect
until it is upon him,
like his pince-nez,
which he shall be searching for,
although he is wearing them,
because it is difficult,
suddenly, singing along, to see.

*"There's just one little thing: a ring.
I don't mean on the phone."*
—**Eartha Kitt**

In lieu of the latkes,
the usual caroling,
and adorable Kazakh
orphans, instead of the crèche
and, *après* ski,
the figgy pudding slash
Kwanzaa stew,
the yuletide blogging,
the tinsel, the garland,
and eight maids eggnogging,
allow me to mince
neither word nor pie
and provide advice
and a list forthwith:
Do not buy and regret,
dear. A diamond
is what to get,
dear. It's extra weight
I'm built to carry.
The starboard lilt,
the opiate
drag on one knuckle,
I'm willing to accommodate
and promise not to buckle
under. Been bottom.
Done shouldered.
It's my time to
plunder, and have a little lovely
something, a nothing-too-modest
something, to set off
all this black
and dazzle the crosshatch
right out of my skin.

O halogen track,
O twinkling lights,
O shining star
upon the highest bough:
you'll soon learn how
to be the ladies in waiting,
stable pony to the thoroughbred,
Martin to a Lewis,
Cathy to a Patty,
mere vein to the carotid—
i.e., to be outwatted.
O Christmas
tree, dear dreidl,
could it be more plainly said?
Some demand the head
upon a platter, others lick
the silver off their spoon.
This childless mother
desires neither moon
nor man but the carat
dangled all this time.
So snare it,
Santa, from that other
sorry cow.
The Baby Jesus phoned,
says I should wear it now.

When Peter Byrne of the '80s synthpop duo, Naked Eyes, played for me
his acoustic cover of k.d. lang's "Constant Craving" in his studio over-
looking Los Angeles, the peacock—not the NBC peacock but a real
peacock among the many on the grounds—opened his fan as if the music
were a potential mate. He strutted and shirred. He shimmied his many
eyes. He'd been drawn to the music, then spotted himself in the sliding
glass doors. He leaned in and turned for us like a Vegas showgirl.
He brought tears to my eyes. When the song was over I could barely
muster, "What a tender version, Peter," though tender wasn't the word
for the primitive if aimless seduction on the lawn. As it happened,
I'd packed my silk shirt, peacock blue, to wear to a poetry reading I was
giving that night, but unlike the peacock and Frank O'Hara, I didn't
intend for anyone to fall into bed with me. Being a purist I wanted my audience
to love the poems—and if they didn't love them, at least they appeared to
enjoy them a little. In Los Angeles, people seem primed for entertainment
at every turn. My uncle-the-former-priest was there, looking like my dead
grandfather. My AP English-teacher-turned-television-executive was there.
I hadn't seen either for twenty-five years. I'd been a grim child—what
would they make of me now? I tossed off words in cadences I'd used
a hundred times. I tried not to think of myself as myself or my words
as my own. I made eye contact as often as possible without losing my place.
From the hills of Palos Verdes, you can see the LA basin fan out like
a poem. Imagine the Hollywood hills as the title, center-justified, the Pacific
lapping its left margin, and all the lights of the city blinking across
its page: Is dotted by arriving flights, Ts crossed by the departing.
Byrne's partner, Rob Fisher, died in 1999. "Always Something
There to Remind Me" was their breakout hit; "Promises, Promises,"
their last. I'd loved my English teacher with a love that measured 7.3
on the Richter scale. My uncle left the priesthood after loving
a fellow parishioner just as hard. In '73, my childhood friend moved
to Palos Verdes; my family moved to California a year later but we never
spoke again. A year after that, I heard that her cousin had slept with my first
boyfriend. We'd believed we'd marry. In '83 my ex-husband and I
married in the Max Factor Chapel in West LA. I can't look at pressed powder

or a freeway exit without thinking of him. The citizens of Palos Verdes
recently circulated a petition urging city officials to remove the city's peacocks
by any means necessary. There's always something we almost always want.
When we see ourselves in each other's eyes the craving stops but only
for the moment it takes for the applause to die down, for the Hollywood sign
to be shrouded in smog again, for a promise to be made or broken, for the cursor
to strut from left to right, before it struts away.

his sweet
encephalitic peonies repel fauns about
as well as they keep ants out
of their own petals. It
was the height
of summer when mine got
in. First I heard a horse trot
by, then the garden gate
snapped shut;
when I heard what
sounded like a hoof hit
every stair-round to my room I thought
I must be dreaming. But
he was no dream. The sheer heat
of him convinced me of that.
I saw the moon lit
often, then put out, in sweat
that rashed across his brow. He was stout,
so winded a bit,
and like any creature on its hind legs, immediate-
ly imposing, yet
exposed somehow too: I felt I ought
to look away. He had a set
of pipes on him! He positively billowed, as if he might
inflate
beyond all help, a loosed issuant some knight
let go of, breaking hell loose down the road. I admit
I panicked and fell for him. It's easy to forget
oneself in the presence of myth. And let
us keep in mind what
gods—even minor ones—are famous for: their kit
bag of tricks, delusions, spells. Mine brought
plenty with him, complete
with smoke and mirrors. I ate
it up and spoon-fed him illusions I was expert at:

maiden pity, mock out-
rage, sometimes Lucy, half White
Witch to his bogus Mr. Tumnus rout-
ine. I never said I was blameless. The ultimate
foolishness is to treat
a body like your baby, lover, parent, pet
when he's a sat-
yr pure and simple. Who can compete
with the wood nymphs? Loot
a cosmology to suit
yourself and it
loots you in return. My advice is. . . . But wait.
My purpose here is not
to convince you of anything. It's much too late
for that already, and while my inclination might
once have been to try, to make a joke, or to write
the greater deities a puling little note
like "Next time, send less man, more goat,"
that's no more remedy, I realize now, than Pliny's herbal fix-it
was. I guess you could say I quit.
Like the rain did tonight
for instance. Its patterned quiet,
whispered rhyme, quite
suddenly gone. Like a fate
you thought
was yours, a minute
lost, a mate.
I've got a new Olympus to create.

File under: Inevitability of: Death,
Taxes (unless you're my father),
Orgasm (unless you're my mother).
Everyone my age not Lasiked gone
Progressive, making them sound entirely more
Bolshevik than they're interesting enough to be.
Not that they aren't progressive (they've met gay people)
And even a little red (where their legs chafe),
But they aren't the young
People they were. Who is,
Except for the young people?

To sum up:
Squirrel carcass on highway
A half a mile ahead: good.
Tuckpoint on skyline, fish scales
Downriver, Blimp over Bismarck:
Good, good, good.
Eyeliner: bad.
Splinter: very bad.
Price tag: catastrophic.

So when the baby chimp at The Nature Center
Grabs my hair by its roots with one
Hand and bitch-slaps me with the other,
Knocking my EvolutionEyes 2.0 readers
(Classic demi-lune lenses in imitation abalone frames)
With a racket to the floor, I can't help
But think: schoolyard: walking the perimeter of,
At recess, only I dutifully receding,
To the vanishing point,
While observing—my vision was perfect
Then—well, you.

Re: schoolyard:
Was it mica in the asphalt that made it sparkle so?
File under:
Skip it.

So when the teenage bureaucrat at the Department of Motor Vehicles
Asks, without looking up, if my address, hair color, eye color, height,
Weight, and organ donation plans remain the same, I answer simply
Yes. And when she announces that I do not need
Corrective lenses in order to drive—
Despite my reluctance to press my forehead against the dingy
Foam pad that activates the light box for the eye exam
(May I borrow a Kleenex, please?)
And my suggestions that the DMV require
A breathalyzer test and proof of insurance on site—I think:
How far I've come.
File under: Maturity, Perspective.
My readers smashed, I cannot see
If my new photo's bad or good, but I can guess.
I am these days infrequently surprised.
When I want to cry I do;
It helps to moisturize.

To sum up:
I could read your stupid T-shirt
From a basement in Iowa,
But I cannot see the salt
On my tomato; I wouldn't know
That child at recess if she were
Standing under my nose, and best of all,
Neither would you, you old fuck,
Not without your glasses.

If it's been ten times it's been forty-five
I've checked the man out in the car behind
mine, teeth bared, laughing in my rearview.

I cannot stop myself from watching him,
sun full on his face. He's all alone—
we are, among our fellow rush commuters—

and then it dawns on me: it's Mr. Cahill
from sixth grade, my first male teacher (heart,
be still!), who taught sex ed to us in '69,

in Catholic school, til someone narked and he
was gone for good. Those days, we venerated
the venereal, reciting sex words right

out loud: Vagina, Penis, Testes, Clit,
plain as the state capitals up and down
each aisle. I lived for the sight of him. And he,

for kindergarten teacher Miss Appell,
who had no sexual parts as far
as we could tell. He liked the shy girls best,

the ones my mom called "pretty on the inside,"
the kind a man could marry. I'd wished to be
the other kind. Then Mr. Cahill changed

all that. And here he is, returned at last,
past middle age, full head of hair, his teeth
intact, gleeful at the wheel of a Honda

Civic, red (Father always said
he was a Communist); and sure enough,
when traffic moves he whips around me faster

35

than you'd think a Civic could. I can't
keep up. O rebel hero: Fellatio,
Intercourse, Cunnilingus, Fuck.

How could we know a tattle then could get
you sent to Nam? He drove too fast there, learned
to like talk radio almost as much

as rock and roll. What strikes his funny bone
this morning would be just another shock
jock talking trash. Sex has turned us rich

or dead or funny, but it turns nobody
bad, as Sister Carol said I'd be
if I kept mum. Love does that, Mr. C.

Inside. Love made a potty-mouth of me.

Tell me if you've heard this one before:
Guy walks into a bar with a duck down his pants,
Says, *One for me and one for my friend here.*
Barkeep says, *That's no friend, that's my wife.*

Guy walks into a bar with a duck down his pants.
A priest, a rabbi, and a minister
Say, *Barkeep, that's no duck, that's proof
Of the existence of God.*

A priest, a rabbi, and a minister
Put together can't tell one good joke.
God knows this
But He cannot forgive them for it.

*Wherever two or more are gathered in a joke,
There is love,* He says. We hear this
But we cannot forgive Him for it.
Suddenly, crashing through the saloon doors,

There is love. And just as He'd said, we know it
By its blonde hair and dead babies.
Suddenly, crashing through the saloon doors,
What's black and white and re(a)d all over.

By its blonde hair and dead babies,
He says, *Barkeep, thou shalt know thy duck.*
What's black and white comes crashing through the door.
Stop me if you've heard this one before.

I will concentric awaken,
a Werther supine in his turquoise granary,
bored B-I-G with this life.

I will bumble my vellum inadequacy,
mythic, atonal, allay.
I will awaken umbrella,

work smartest not hardest,
toast yesteryears with quinine, adultery, and snub.
And if ever you were in my arms again,

if ever happiness
and the freedom to remain e-rect were restored,
I would gladly eat

your Cartesian hat, coleus, quincunx,
my Ceres, my sled.
I would concentric awaken,

a Kowalski to his soup,
Comanche to your Sputnik, all
shameful lacquers and wiley enhancement—

because lesion I love you.
It's me rap-rapping your Spenserian windows,
an oeuvre moving offshore.

Hi Hi Hi

A tub is that which would be king,
But we must cease to praise shallow water.
Too many baths are conceited. And then
There's that bathtub-addled Moon,
For whom Des Moines gleams like a suitor
Waving his wampum of porcelain and brass.
Drawn, now, to chrome and fiberglass,
She feels the pull of neither sea nor stream.
The lakes have lost their glistening.
There are, instead, these sudsy ponds of men,
These steaming spas of marble and tile,
An immersed depression, laved,
And children mewling for their no-tears shampoo
When we're clean out, nothing to tide us over.

She was born, like so many of us,
With a monkey on her back.
Her family said, As long as she's healthy . . .
And took them home in the car.

The monkey on her back
Grew as she did, strong and smart.
They learned to drive a car,
Went away to a good college.

They married a Mr. Reginald N. Smart,
Worked up until the first baby,
Worked again when the last left for college.
They'd been a good mother, everyone agreed.

But when the first grandchild was born
With a monkey on his back,
The children blamed their mother. Everyone agreed
It was time for an intervention.

The monkey turned his back
To the family, which made it hard to hold on.
In time he fell and fractured a vertebra,
And that was the beginning of the end.

He tried to hold on, but it was hard.
In time she told him to just let go.
That was the end of the end for them,
And they died, like so many of us.

. . . .

The saints know what to do
with their hands: lily lamb staff mundi.
If it's a handful
they take it on. They were born
to take it, to die
taking it. And how they suffer
the slings and arrows, the little children,
shoulder the burden and roll
their eyes, literally, heavenward
in a private joke with Jesus:
Eli Eli,
Deus ex.
Actors each in the anatomical theater,
hands aloft on cue:
This is my hobby. Eat it . . .

"Note. This Angel, who is now become a Devil,
is my particular friend: we often read the Bible
together in its infernal or diabolical sense, which
the world shall have if they behave well."
—*William Blake,* Marriage of Heaven and Hell

. . . .

INTERVIEWER: You are said to favor a soft shoe, an open door, the embryo before a single sex gets hold . . .

ELIJAH: No doors on the valleys. No doors on the skies. Cave mouths: open.

INTERVIEWER: In fact, you were a cave dweller yourself for many years . . .

ELIJAH: Because a world is all entrance for the young and happy animal. That is what I was, and gamin fast. Even the resistance of the wind and of the river pleased me then. I started kind-hearted, not knowing one future from the next. YWHA had other plans.

INTERVIEWER: The gift of prophecy.

ELIJAH: Yes. To prophecy. But first, a test.

INTERVIEWER: The Angel of Death.

ELIJAH: Aren't we all? The Law of Heaven is to destroy what it cannot harvest. The rest is harvested. But such knowledge arrived for me . . . truantly. The point is, I could have delivered the final blow, and would have, but God had further use of Death. He likes his prophets like his angels: strong and obedient. Olive tree. Oil lamp. And so I became a wearer of sackcloth and I smote the waters with my mantle. Fire issued from my mouth when I spoke, and I shut up the sky for drought, raised up the dead for widows, etc. As it was prophesied, Elisha, my successor, my son in all ways but one, stayed with me until the Lord's whirlwind consumed me and I rode the fiery chariot to heaven.

INTERVIEWER: Translated from earth to heaven.

ELIJAH: I left no written record here nor keep one there.

INTERVIEWER: In this context, I mean translated as in to leave the world without dying. You're one of only a very few to be translated.

ELIJAH: But language is everywhere. Michael, for instance: his body sprouted with tiny saffron hairs, each containing a million faces and mouths and as many tongues imploring in a million dialects the pardon of Allah. Suffering has both face and voice. Death has neither.

INTERVIEWER: I'm afraid I'm not making myself clear. . . . Allah?

ELIJAH: Language everywhere. And odours, which are the prayers of the saints. My nephew Methuselah smelled of spring for years after his birth. For nine hundred sixty-nine years he lived. All those words and not one prophetic. One's throat becomes parched either way. Have you a cup of something for me, dear?

is the suitcase
as a frame, subway
grate, trap
door, rabbit
hole, bottomless
pit, as Mary
Poppins's carpet
bag only Mary
doesn't lift
floor lamps
out of it you
look down
onto reeds
undulating
in a tide pool
a little brackish
maybe near a
cave entrance look
starfish, anemones
aquatic plants
emitting greenish
gas you want
to go down
there & aren't
able to
stop looking
& then you see
the big waxy
legs with black
human hairs
waving on
them & the little
waxy hairless

legs higher
up you haven't
seen legs this
deliberately
torso-less since
Icarus nosedived
into the Aegean
in Brueghel's painting
which you know
only because of
the Auden
poem "Musée des
Beaux Arts"
about folks
minding their own
beeswax in
Musée des
Wax Poetic
we see how
Art begets
Art & Father
begets Child but
once you open
that kettle of
suitcase—
Astonish me!
Diaghilev instructed
his company at
the Ballets Russes—
you can't ever
climb back out.

It is amply documented that the Ice Age vegetarian
ground sloth once lived in Ohio and other forested
areas of what is now known as North America.
Standing upright to feed on trees, the sloth reached
heights of fifteen to twenty feet before dying out
with tens of thousands of other species as a result
of climate change or, more likely, human intervention.
In 1799, Thomas Jefferson, third president and the first
U.S. citizen credited with studying fossils, contemplated
the sloth's remains, declaring it a great catlike carnivore.
In 1822, it was, unlike some of his offspring, given his name:
Megalonyx jeffersoni, or Giant Claws Jefferson. Wired
to the throat of the model is a small unarticulated bone.
We all have one, said our museum guide, *the hyoid, or*
tongue bone, which allows us to speak and is almost
always found broken on victims of strangulation. But
they're not saying, he snickered, *either way.*

So which mammalian fuck-up list produced
the platypus, produced the bird-billed, flat-foot, erstwhile
beavers dressed like ducks for Halloween?
Crepuscular and nipple-less,
they suckle hatchlings in the changeling dusk—

Diaphanously the god-swan boned
a married chick and she begot two eggs,
neither good. The launching of a thousand ships ensued.
Homer never saw a platypus,
though in his dreams he may have heard them growl,
a noise between a gurgle and a hiss.
The males are venomous. A plural
form of platypus does not exist.

I would have preferred it if he'd followed his
original ambition and become an architect.
—Paula Hitler, younger sister, late 1945

When Kierkegaard died of complications from a childhood
fall from a tree—a Dutch Elm in Denmark,
itself an early casualty of the famous
Dutch Elm Disease, and The Homesickness Unto Death—
the fruit didn't land far from Linz and the Realschule
Wittgenstein and Hitler attended together in 1904.

By then, Stern-Halma—a game played not with language
but for all the marbles just the same—
was a popular pastime. It's not hard to imagine
bookish Ludwig and dreamy Adolf as boys bent over
the board, a star with six points, arguing over which
version of the game to play, either "hop across" or "capture."

That year, Regine Olsen's body was buried near her beloved,
long-dead Søren in Copenhagen. Kierkegaard, his hair
like a Pentecostal flame, could never quite take the leap
in love he could in faith. All love, he wrote to her, like all knowledge,
is remembrance. He later wrote an analysis on the nature of despair.

Wittgenstein possessed perfect pitch, but lacked the genius
for music his three brothers, all suicides, once shared.
Hitler was a skilled watercolorist of Viennese scenery and landmarks,
but was twice rejected by the Academy of Fine Arts. By 1910
he was living in a homeless shelter selling hand-painted postcards
    to tourists.

In 1939, the Wittgensteins bought their freedom from the Nazis
for a fortune equal to 2% of the Austrian National Gold Reserves.
In 1941, the American Milton Bradley Company acquired the rights
to Chinese Checkers, the game originally known as Stern-Halma.
In 1963, Levinas criticized Kierkegaard's "leap of faith" as a type of
violence.
In 1970, Hitler's remains were exhumed, cremated, and dumped into
the Elbe.

Wittgenstein called Kierkegaard—a man with many pseudonyms—
"a saint."
Kierkegaard called his journals his "most trusted confidant."
"Søren hearts Regine," he may have written there;
but he could never bring himself to marry her.
The name Hitler is from the German, meaning "shepherd,"
though Wagner's grandchildren affectionately called him Uncle Wolf.

My room is in Angers, France.
A rind grows around it.
A bear sleeps under the window.
My room is in Grandioser, Illinois,

The Painted Desert, Arizona,
Big Savage Mountain, USA.
I have a runaway truck ramp
In that room, I have plenty

Of local color. My room is in
Caliban, Mass., Indigo, Japan,
Apocrypha, OK. Sundays we grill
Panhandle-Hellenic, and feel the residual

Blues. Xerox the corn & you'll
Find us. Cut out the pictures of fog.
You won't get a proper pantoum
In my room, but I'll paint you

A portrait of lonely from memory:
A nest of red bees are the baby
Mice, a roof made of birds
Is the Steller's Jay laughing.

My room's on the corner of Castle
& Liberty, Wormwood & 116th.
You've seen the signs everywhere.
My room is in Angers, France.

*"I should not say, of Taglioni, exactly that she dances,
but that she laughs with her arms and legs, and that
if she takes vengeance on her present oppressors, she
will be amply justified by the* lex Talionis.*"*
—Edgar Allan Poe, 1849

. . . .

Will the little hunchback ever learn
To dance, I asked the master, yes, and would
Again—her ostrich limbs, giraffe comportment
Laughable and, worse, a blow to dance
No genius costumer could mask. Plus,
She was a bitch. Entitled. Heiress
Taglioni. Comptesse Gilbert de Voisins.
Your horror story man, a Monsieur Poe,
Reported her divorce, a *separation
De corps* less surgical than most,
For that newspaper . . . what's it called?
The theater made of it! The two had lived
Apart for years by then; we did not think
Her son was his. All families are dramatic,
I suppose.
                    I was a Taglioniste
Also, in my way, as generous, more
Perhaps, with vinegar in her water glass
As mine: it helped to keep us all *sylphide.*
The Evening Mirror! Foolish name! What can
One see within a looking glass at night?
Precisely nothing. Why not call it *Nothing?*
That would be French.
                              She took the ballet down
To darkness she alone disturbed, what light,
A light of arms and ankles pushing off
The music like a too-devoted pet.
No one could call Marie a natural;

The supernatural was more her style.
And dead now in an unmarked grave, she seems
The same Marie to me: plain, pale,
Round-shouldered like a pearl, or like the speck,
The agitant, that would become the pearl.

you slayed
in your starling
suit at midnight,

the only goldfish
in the castle.
How aqueous backyards

were back then,
how silver the
streets, like a

bevel of thermometer
still slick with
your tongue. You

bet you were
fluent in exhale.
You were just that

gone.

Caramel of the upstairs
of the morning & nighttime
little breath
acrobat
come hither & climb

Caramel it's bedtime
caramel & more cream
stubble in the snow
dream please
small sing to me

I will open my door
if you come to my door
on your pink toes
small cara-
mel of the morning I will

Because rosehips swell redly on
  the canes of the climbers
    you tied back with twine
      to four nails rusted
        in the silver green siding,
  I fear.
Because mud rut in the alley,
  all gravel, wisteria, lame
    dog, and dryer sheet.
Because red barn twist-falling
  like the shot cowboy in a melodrama,
    and the mellow drama of autumn
      with its strata of maple leaves
        that could bury a man
          with a rake and his boots on.
Because the frost,
  I fear,
    earth heaving like my chest
      that time.
Because Hades is, evidently, filled
  with china, none of it matched,
    and the night air breeds bats
      that slip in on the breeze
        and the day air, a cardinal's song
          I'm bound to forget the words to.
Because the thirty-two windows tall enough to walk through,
  their glazier dead a hundred years,
    I fear.
Because five windows of average size.
Because of all eight doors, three chimneys,
  their carpenter and mason.
Because not a line is level
  or an angle true.
Because no two measurements are equal.

Because, if it rolls, it will roll on those floors,
the oak floors with their intricate knowledge
of geometry, astronomy, entomology;
and the oak doors with their transoms,
the oak banister trained to my hand,
coffin turn at the top.
Because, among its many severities, its levity:
the mantels' codpiece medallions,
staircase finial coming off in your hand
like a Christmas movie,
the Eat-Me Drink-Me radiators,
a basement missing
and the superfluous door that isn't,
knob turning and turning and turning.
Because it took, likewise, a comic genius
to hang a ship's chandelier
in the galley dining room
of a landlocked house.
Because sewing needles between the floorboards,
small vines climbing
the wallpaper.
Because alphabet and box fans.
Because the pink. Because the blue.
Because the acorn rains and the petal snows.
Because the old woman
who is always talking
tells the old man
who is never listening,
I visited the old house today.
Because their children's children.
Because their marbles, cirrus clouds
caught inside.
Because in the future,
in my memory,
these rooms shall live
a great deal longer than I shall live,
I fear.

Because the stench of black walnut,
   the lilac that never bloomed
    and the forsythia that did,
      the peonies and roses
        pink and red against the silver-green siding
          we painted ourselves
            in the color we had to have
Because of its name, which was Solitary.

The crucifix bent nearly parallel
to earth, the plastic cherubs poised, mid-lim-
bo, under each arm of the cross's T

were meant to make the unseen visible:
X marks the spot where Jesus called our Jim-
bo home, and were erected solemnly,

in prayer, while semis shuddered half a mile
away and small things moved inside the berm
grass. They were not then the sorry junk we see,

ephemera nodding toward eternity,
til nodding off completely, once and for all.
The highway is a public place and we,

a people dying for a sign. Simple-
ton angels posed in imbecile poses: some-
one thought they'd keep the lost one company,

like giving to a fussy child a doll
to help it sleep, to dream the pleasant dreams
of the oblivious. And look! a teddy

bear for Baby, wreath for Mom, and twistied
to the fence they raised when Junior jumped
the overpass, helium balloons.

This crap from Wal-Mart could outlast us all,
which in our grief is no small com-
fort, since death lasts so much longer, and has no form.

ACKNOWLEDGMENTS

I am grateful to the editors who originally published these poems:

" 'I should not say, of Taglioni . . .' ": *Barrow Street*

" 'And I took the little book . . .' " and "Nostophobia": *Center*

"Postmodern Penelope at Her Loom Pantoum" and "Womb to Tomb Pantoum":
   Cincinnati Review

"Ontology and the Platypus" and "Lunacy": *Colorado Review* ("Ontology and the
   Platypus" also appeared as a limited edition broadside from the Center for
   Book Arts, New York)

" 'What she could do . . .' ": *Columbia Magazine*

"Butter": *Columbia Poetry Review*

" 'No cakes for us . . .' " and "Diadem": FIELD

" 'How long, O Lord, how long?' " and " 'Note. This Angel, who is now become a
   Devil . . .' ": *Flights*

"Road Memorial": *The Kenyon Review*

"Leap of Faith": *The Laurel Review*

"SPAM": *The Los Angeles Review*

" '69" and "Constant Craving": *New Ohio Review*

"Bad Patch": *Northwest Review*

"Darling," and "Design for the Costume of a Minor Divinity": *Pilot*

" 'God helps those . . .' ": *Ploughshares*

"Three, Becoming Spring" and "Progressive Lenses": *Poetry Northwest*

"Lament" and "Now You See It": *Pool* ("Now You See It" also appeared in
   The Ohio State University Alumni Magazine)

"Saloon Pantoum" and " 'There's just one little thing . . .' ": *Slate*

"Pontoon Pantoum #505" and "Go to Your Room, Pantoum": *Smartish Pace*
   ("Pontoon Pantoum #505" also appeared on versedaily.com)

I am grateful to the College of Humanities at The Ohio State University for awarding
me an Arts and Humanities Grant-in-Aid (Manuscript Preparation), which helped to
defray the cost of the cover illustration.

For their encouragement, advice, and many kindnesses, my thanks also to Angie
Estes, Michelle Herman, Scott Hightower, Chris Howell, Pablo Tanguay, and David
Young.

ABOUT THE AUTHOR

. . . .

Kathy Fagan is the author of three previous collections of poetry: *The Raft*, winner of the National Poetry Series; MOVING & ST RAGE, winner of the 1998 Vassar Miller Prize for Poetry; and *The Charm* (2002). Her work has appeared in *The Paris Review*, FIELD, *Ploughshares*, *The Colorado Review*, *The Laurel Review*, and *The New Republic*, among many other publications, and has been anthologized in collections such as *Poet's Choice*, *The Extraordinary Tide*, and *Writing Poems*. The recipient of fellowships from the Ingram Merrill Foundation, the NEA, and the Ohio Arts Council, Fagan teaches in the MFA program at The Ohio State University, where she also serves as poetry editor for *The Journal*.

Photo by A. Estes.